... Tragedy

A

born Survivor

Struggling

Against all Odds

Kruella ~ A Daughter's Tale

By

S.K. Hope

Xx Dedicated to

My loving Grandmother

Mildred Haynes Xx

Acknowledgments

I would like to thank those who have contributed, confided, giving me strength and determination to write this book. I hope this will empower others to free themselves from the bondages of past and with the release of the truth they will come to realise they are not at fault but in fact the blame lies with many others.

To all those who have been afflicted with eating disorders, depression, self-harm and O.C.D please do not suffer in silence there is so much help and advice on offer, never feel ashamed.

I wrote this book to help and let you know that I am a survivor and what I have experienced does not define who I am and that you can overcome. I have this found writing this very painful, and emotional whilst cathartic.

I was not responsible for what happened to me and I feel those who were involved should have to accept some accountability for their negligent actions, which has gone onto to leave a detrimental lasting effect on my life but has also made me a courageous strong determined black woman.

Contents

1. Prologue
2. Alma Road
3. The Firm
4. Home Alone
5. My Name is Tallulah
6. Toy Stories
7. The Colour Purple
8. Grange Hill
9. Back to School
10. Nightmare on South Street
11. What's Love Got To Do With It
12. Bugs Bunny to Beauty Queen
13. I'm Coming Out
14. Panic Room

15. Touched By Angels

16. Family Talk

17. My Stepdad Tony

18. Epilogue

19. Help Lines & Helpful Organisations

Prologue

I remember being so excited for school, I had been up from very early and I made sure, because I did not wanna miss it. I must have been up for about 6:30am; I think of looking out of the big front room window with the bright sunshine and white nets with heavy curtains, as you could see the school gates back then.

My birth Mother who I will refer to in this book mostly as Yvonne was never an early riser, she was an alcoholic. I spent a lot of time alone in my childhood before my little sister came along and I barely recollect my other siblings as they were removed and placed into social services care.

You never woke Yvonne when she was sleeping unless it was very urgent, or someone was at the door, which was a bit of problem when I had school but I took a chance "Mum...mum I got school today"...... Usually she would rouse with a ferocious "What!!" followed by a resounding kissing of the teeth which would lead one to quickly retreat downstairs and await for the sound of pounding creaking footsteps on the staircase hoping to god she had woken up in good mood which wasn't very often if not rare.

We may have been late for school as I call to mind going in, in the afternoon after dinner time the bell had rang and the din of the school kids had faded. Yvonne had got me a denim suit for my first day jeans and jacket but it was cheap tat….market stall tat probably from Ridley road market in Dalston.

The school was literally across the road from where we lived in a maisonette and Yvonne had got me ready, washed, fed and dressed no excitement, no chatter, but more of a chore. I can honestly say I cannot remember Yvonne ever hugging me or showing much motherly affection towards me from a young age.

We left and were about to cross the road when the zipper of the jacket had come off in my hand and I showed her innocently, with that she yanked me up shouting blaming me for breaking it but to this day I remember it just came away. She was trying hastily to rectify it to no avail. I cannot quote exactly what she said but it was something like "Why you fucking touch it" and with that, she gave me one slap to the face, which rang out through to my ears.

Yvonne had long nails and one scratched the left side cheek near my nose, which started to bleed, we proceeded to cross the road and entered into the school playground. Yvonne was a fast walker and I had difficulty keeping up and I was in shock, I tried to talk but I could not….

I was just numb.

My face had started bleeding slightly with my tears stinging running into the wound. We had reached the main school doors and Yvonne pressed the buzzer on noticing my tears and blood Yvonne found a tissue and wiped away the evidence. The door opened the teacher welcomed me in "Hello Sharron" with a big smile and with that Yvonne was gone.

I was sitting in the classroom room brightly coloured with books, toys, and crayons wondering what I had done to be have been struck in the face.

I pondered if other kids had a mum like mine or if they had, had a first day like mine. That is my first memory of Alma Road School I was approximately 5 years old.

Alma Road

Before we moved to Enfield we lived in south London, Brockley, which I barely think of except it was another maisonette. I am not sure what happened but we ended up in Palmers Green a halfway house hostel, it was for battered women.

It was awful dark, dank and smelly with little room for manoeuvre and it was full of other families with their kids. We had our own room but had to share the amenities and the toys, which involved interacting with other children.

It was here that I first encountered racism from a family who made my life a misery whilst I was there.

We then moved to Alma Road and I was so relieved to be rid of the racist clan only to my horror find out later they had moved into the block straight in front of us. This family made mine and some on the street a living hell. They would chase you on their bikes until you ran home scared, shout abuse and be quite menacing. However, it abruptly came to an end one day in the summer holidays when it finally came to a family friend getting a boy their age to deal with the matter.

That evening or sometime later, the youths fight evolved and a brawl involving adults erupted, the police were called and shortly after the family moved away to great sighs of relieve from the whole street. Generally, we had to deal with a lot of racism at that time there were only a few black families on the street, six to be exact.

There was always some form of friction on the street every day and the police were frequently seen visiting various addresses. Alma Road was notorious for a whole host of catastrophes from gangs, drugs, murders, prostitution, tramps, drunks, suicides, glue sniffers and paedophiles.

One day the whole maisonette block, where we lived was raided; our disabled next-door neighbour had been dealing dodgy stolen videos and televisions, which he had sold to the block amongst other things. The Police had the block under surveillance for several months and

Yvonne was arrested along with a fair few visitors in our house due to large amounts of Cannabis seized. I was not at all impressed as it was a school day and it was my little sisters' birthday, which we spent most of it in Enfield Town police station.

I never really got invited to school friend's birthday parties because everyone knew who Yvonne was, the stories and rumours plus my clothes came from a generation of cast offs. And even when I was luckily enough to be invited Yvonne would usually always say "No".

My distant family relatives who felt sorry for our plight would always come annually with their various hand me downs of shoes and clothes justifying their reasoning why we never were invited out anywhere and them feeling like they done their bit for charity. Everything was second hand which I hated with a passion especially, after I caught a Verruca.

Growing up there I soon realised 57, it was literally a dumping ground, I mean ponders end to me equalled "Dead End" ponders end, nothing good came out of it accept bad luck experiences, tales and quite a few deaths actually. Those that could saved and left, onto pastures new with a fresh start. Others stayed out of no choice or revelled in the history and misfortune of the place.

Most of the neighbours were scared of Yvonne or thought she was mad as she never conformed in fact I would say frankly she was somewhat eccentric with some complex mental health issues.

She also had her fair share of arguments and fights on the street and would often frequent many of the pubs in the local area namely the Alma, the Falcon, the Railway and the Horse and Dray.

Yvonne would visit daily with me and my younger sister outside, my baby sister in the buggy and me pacified with a Coco Cola in a bottle those days, a multi coloured striped straw along with a green packet of Golden Wonder Cheese and Onion Crisps.

She would stay there until closing until she was so inebriated that someone would eventually have to carry her and walk us home with my sister fallen asleep in the buggy. It was always usually a white man who would take us back, sometimes a stranger taking his chances and ending up staying. Drinking and laughing into the late hours of the night and in the morning, they were gone.

This would happen on a regular and I began to despise men, white men, men in general.

I am aware some of the neighbours did call social services but others never and knew exactly what was going on and chose to do nothing. And nothing was really done, they came spoke to Yvonne checked us over and that was it, we were never removed from her care.

Yvonne did eventually manage to catch a Fisherman, I was around four at the time and my baby sister was six months. I disliked him but he weren't like the rest, he took us both to our first fair ground, gave us pocket money, treats and showed a genuine interest and love for Yvonne. He stayed around for over twenty years and done his best by us but that's another chapter.

The Firm

Yvonne came to England when she was Thirteen years old from George Town, Guyana and from what I gathered; she was very reluctant to come, her mother having left her alone for a while with family members who mistreated her. On arrival to Britain, she was mocked for her Guyanese accent and was fighting in a middle class school after relentless bullying and taunts.

Her mother, my lovely grandmother was working as a limbo dancer touring Germany and in her later years worked with young people as a youth worker.

I think my grandmother was very disappointed in Yvonne's less than ambitious achievements and I do remember my mother being bailed out time and time again, and my Nan being very upset indeed. I know Yvonne was annoyed with her mother as she did once have aspirations to be an actress and after my grandmother's death a letter from Pinewood's studios inviting her to audition had been found which Yvonne never did receive.

She had five children, two boys and three girls with me being a twin, whose other half never made it, very premature and was the second from last. I can only imagine it must have been very chaotic, Yvonne had five children from four different men and only one of them she married.

I look back at me and my little sister growing up together, and our fathers whom were friends co-incidentally, visiting sporadically during our younger years. This caused a lot of contention and jealousy between us especially if the other had been given a better gift.

The elder siblings would visit most weekends and we would be happy as they always came with food, sweets and toys if they could. When it was time for them to go, it would be tears, and pleadings not to leave as we knew what the coming long week ahead would entail neglect, hunger and boredom….

Yvonne at some stage was a grafter and done whatever she needed to do in order to feed and clothe herself and her children, she was also a fierce fighter, brawler, fraudster and a thief. She had been a visitor at HMP Holloway, even giving birth to one of her children whilst in custody.

In our house, it was sink or swim, every man, woman and child for him or herself and do whatever to survive. If I got beat up and returned home crying Yvonne would tell me to get out and "Beat the fuckers" or "I gone beat yah rass if you come back crying again".

We were starved on so many levels, but predominately love and affection. We were a burden and when she was in a bad mood she would let us know, by throwing things and shouting savagely, "You set of ungrateful bitches, Alyah cunts, what did I do to deserve you bastards? I wish Alyah dead scunt and I had an abortion".

It became quite regular these obscene outbursts, in the end and as a defence mechanism, in private we would mock her word for word and take the anguish out of it.

Deprived of a hug, cuddle or enquiry into our general wellbeing, as sisters we supported each other, sleeping in the same bed and we would bang our heads in unison onto the pillow and shake our feet to go to sleep with a made up melody, we would create together. I think it was like a self-comfort, yeah it was fucked up.

In later years, all the siblings came home to live with Yvonne, those were the better days we knew there would be food plentiful and we wouldn't be left alone too long if Yvonne decided to do a disappearing act. She worshipped Mecca Bingo and dreamt of winning big but when she did, all it accomplished was arguments as Yvonne favoured the Sons over her daughters and it was blatantly obvious to those around.

Family and siblings do of course argue but I never understood why it would always turn into violence. I remember my older sister had acquired shall we say a very expensive Armani woollen jumper and my brother had it having borrowed it for some time and she now wanted it back.

It was a school evening and I heard fighting going on upstairs, he did not want to give it back, her own jumper and so the argument escalated and turned physical moving from upstairs to down with my little sister screaming her head off uncontrollably and me just quiet that's how I went, we did have some comfort though, my sisters friend and brother's ex was there too and she tried to console us. Yvonne was in the kitchen, she got a broom handle, and my brother was forcibly removed from the house. And as for the jumper he put his foot through it and that was the end of the expensive Armani jumper.

Having the older siblings back made the house super busy they would go to the local youth centre and then they would all pile round to ours, pranks, smoking, movies and listening to music. This would also include school days and I would find myself often side stepping sleeping bodies in the front room looking for my stuff for school in the morning.

Yvonne liked it when the house was full that is when she would be at her most dangerous. She would embarrass us in front of people, accusing me of stuff I had not even done. I remember the front room was packed and she just started hitting me for no reason I was crying shouting, "I ain't done nothing" my older sister had to intervene frantically explaining I had not done nothing and to "Leave her". I believe later my older sister came to realise that Yvonne was quite a nasty horrible person. My big sister always got involved to protect us and it would result in some violent exchange between her and Yvonne. There was never any apology, I came to recognise when the house was packed stay away or become a target.

She would use favouritism by taking my little sister to functions and leaving me or bringing something new back for my sister only. It was noticed but It did not bother me after a while I just got used to staying behind. When she was, nice I would get to go out on an adventure with her selling black pudding and fish cakes, in pubs and clubs, sometimes late at night and I would end up missing days off at school. Probably thinking about logically I was brought along to keep her safety men knowing she had a young child in tow men would be less inclined to approach her in sexual way.

My little sister got to stay up later with the downstairs crowd even though I was older than she was, and I was sent to bed early. They favoured her as she was light, fairer, cute looking whilst I was dark, black, goofy and often reminded of my faults in taunts and put downs.

It was hard to accept but I took it and gave it to the street kids when I got upset or started fights so I could relinquish all this anger and torment that had stored up within me.

Sometimes our sibling's mates would look us after, which weren't cool, as they would make me and my sister spar and fight each other for their own fun and amusement, which was actually abuse too.

If yah done bird, hustled, smoked it was ok everything was cool. Stuff came into the house, people socialised, meetings were held, deals were made, and that was the firm at 57.

Home Alone

I really did love going to Alma School it holds a lot of positive memories and it was the one place I was guaranteed a meal every day. We were rarely given the stable three meals a day, and we were always hungry. So glad the school was close to where we lived as I don't know how we would of managed considering Yvonne did not get up regularly to do our breakfast and make sure we were washed, dressed and brushed our teeth.

When we did have meal times, it was usually late and stale food, which my sister and I would saturate in tomato ketchup to mask the awful taste and smell. We were made to finish our plate before we could leave the table, so often a plan hatched between us. We would stuff our mouths with food, empty it into the toilet, and then flush it when it was full to not raise her suspicions.

With the stale hot milk and the fresh Frostie's it was a bit more challenging. We would have to eat the breakfast and then the body's natural reaction would be to retch, run to the bathroom and vomit.

She knew we did not like some of the food, clearly, after it had been sitting there cold for several hours, that she prepared and that it was inedible but she didn't care often responding negatively "your gon eat this fucking food before you leave the table". I would try to avoid certain dinner times by all means, eating out anywhere else I could find.

When she disappeared, it just happened without notice usually on a Monday after she had cashed her benefit book. She would do basic food shopping then she'd be off around six to catch the early evening bingo session and then it would be my responsibility to get us both up in the morning for school. We would make it to school either way too early or more often too late well after the bell had rung, which would be ideal if I hadn't had breakfast due to hunger as I could raid the lunch boxes before they got moved to the lunch area. I always did feel bad when it was lunchtime and half the other school kids shit was missing but on the other hand, at least they got treated to a nice dinner when they got home.

If she went for a few days the electric meter would run out, it ran on fifty pence pieces in those days, and I would never ask our neighbours, and they knew.

My little sister would be sorted in bed or out with Yvonne and I would stand at the end of the street and hope for her to return till way after midnight had past. When it had gotten too dark and I was, sleepy, exhausted of waiting, then I would go to bed and sleep in my school uniform to counteract being late in the morning. I would also have the curtains wide open to shine light into my bedroom from the street lamps outside.

I hated being alone, I hated it even more being alone in the dark there was always something creepy about 57 alma road, I felt like a presence was there, hovering and watching me.

It did not help matters all the inappropriate horror movies about graveyards, zombies, murder and death, which I had no choice but to watch whilst getting my hair braided ready for school. Some strange things had happened in there and Yvonne herself often said she felt people or persons had died in the house.

On this one night, I had stayed up quite late again, waiting for Yvonne to return so we could have light and food, I look back my little sister had fallen asleep. By now, I had gotten into a routine that if I slept in my uniform I would have enough time to get my sister ready, brush teeth, get breakfast or a hot drink with biscuits, and aim not be late.

It must have been between two and three thirty in the morning the bedroom door flung open and the light switched on, Yvonne was shouting and awoke us striking me with a belt, my poor sister had time to scramble under the actual bed for cover and I under the duvet wriggling from the lashes. She was shouting "Alyah nasty who tell you, you could sleep ina yah school clothes". I managed to snake under the bed petrified viewing the soles of her black shoes moving round the room deciding on her next move. I watched as her shoes exited towards the bedroom door before they turned around "Take off your school clothes and get to bed and let me catch you in them again see what will happen" and with that she was gone, the door was shut and neither of us moved until we heard the creaking of her steps going downstairs. If she lost at bingo, she would take it out on us whether we were awake or not she would never take responsibility for her actions.

We got out from under our hiding places and we undressed whispering our cries and not saying a word to each other, getting into bed and creating a melody through tears. If she had only just asked me to explain, it would have been plausible but that was Yvonne all over…….

Strike first and don't ever ask questions.

Both sister and I would be fearful, agitated and frightened at Yvonne's unpredictable behaviour that it eventually led to bedwetting of the sheets and then we could get a beaten for "pissing the bed".

It was even worse in the school holidays and weekends as she started to lock us in and that was awful because we had to climb out the kitchen, bedroom or toilet window, but often we just stayed in as we would get a beating when Yvonne returned and she found out we had left the house. Our friends would knock for us and we would tell them were locked in and they would not believe it.

One weekend we were locked in and we survived on Kellogg's Frostie's with no milk that is all we had. I know the kids went back and told their parents and some would even walk pass by to see if it was true. But as long as our friends came to the window to talk to us, we were ok.

And when we did get the opportunity to play out after doing all the chores in the house it came with its own set of problems. We integrated well with the kids in the neighbourhood; they liked us; however, that could not be said for some of the parents who ostracised us, attempting to force the kids not to play with us.

They would purposely exclude us from parties or play activities at their houses. Treated like pariahs, me and my little sister would be left hankering, looking in from the outside on the doorstep or the door would be closed on us and that was that.

On other occasions neighbours would give out sweets, lollies and blatantly not give us any, with the child given strict instructions not to share with us, some did some didn't and if the worse came to the worst, we would hunt for stale sweets covered with ants but a quick wash and fuck it, we got sweets too.

When the Ice Cream van came in the summer, we would slowly run off and build up the courage to ask Yvonne if we could get a lolly, if we had visitors we got and if not Yvonne had made her own version of ice cream and bought ice popes instead.

The school did know what was going on and called social services on more than one occasion, but they came spoke to Yvonne checked us over and that was it, we were never removed.

My sister recalls the police attending on a weekend and I have a vague memory, we explained that Yvonne had gone and locked us in but they went away and they never came back.

By now, it was obviously clear Yvonne was not parent material and that she should not be in charge of caring for children. Why did the police not immediately remove us on the grounds of neglect? Why did Social services fail us as young children? And why did some of the neighbours not come to our aid?

The first time I tried to kill myself I was approximately eight and a half years old, I was very sad and distraught at the life I was experiencing so I swallowed a penny and it was lodged in my throat. Then I went to bed with the hope that I would be free. Unfortunately, at the time for me, I woke up the next day and I was still alive, I was so downhearted and I started to panic, which started to affect my breathing and actually, I started to choke. My natural instincts and adrenaline kicked in and so I ran down stairs into the kitchen and took a slice of bread, swallowing big clumps of Sunblest followed by a glass of water and then the penny went down, scraping hard as it entered into my system.

I asked god why he let me live and then I acknowledged it must be for good reason I did not die.

My name is Tallulah

Growing up I always enjoyed watching the Saturday matinee, or the afternoon musicals on the television, it was also a form of escapism from the misery. I loved watching films with Elvis Presley, Alfred Hitchcock, Marilyn Monroe, Bette Davis, Joan Crawford, Liza Minnelli, Kenneth Williams, Sid James and other numerous great stars.

The Lion, Witch and Wardrobe by C.S Lewis a book I was able to get lost into and forget the reality of the abysmal real life I was enduring.

I became a bookworm attending the local library most days after school any excuse to avoid going home.

My Nan took me to see a play but this was different, it was a theatrical stage play with black people in it!!!! First time I had seen anything like it, it was wonderful to see black talent and I realised it is not just white people who act black people can too!!! And not just be a maid servant, slave, Zulu or a pair slippers and voice from the Tom & Jerry cartoons.

Mrs Smith was such a lovely Teacher; I wonder what became of her? She felt so sorry for me at times; I could see the pain etched on her face. However, it was at a time when I think the school was too embarrassed and did not want the shame so it went under the radar kind of.

So, when our year found out we were doing "Bugsy Malone" we were all excited, especially me as it was and still is one my favourite films of all time

It was even a bigger shock and surprise when I got cast as "Tallulah", I couldn't believe it....

Black, boney, goofy Sharron got the lead part!!!! Jodie Forster, me her biggest fan!!! We rehearsed nearly every day for weeks and made sure I never missed a day. We laughed and had so much fun and when the performance date came, there was a buzz and all the parents came…even Yvonne made it.

It was a great success!!! Mums and dads were tearful for the effort we had made and Yvonne clapped until she was one of the lasts ones standing. It was one of the best feelings in the world!!!

It was then I realised and it was confirmed….

I want to be an Actress!!!

That same week Mrs Smith sent me home with a message for Yvonne, that she wanted to speak with her about an opportunity.

Turns out the teacher had spoken to a friend after the play about my performance and they wanted to see me.

Mrs Smith told her about Bodens, that there was a place for me to attend, but my heart sank when she started to mention money and how much it would cost. I saw the lack of interest drain from Yvonne's face.

I even tried desperately to contact my estranged father to see if he could help but he was always busy, with the next 3:30pm race at Kempton, or the greyhound race at Walthamstow dog track. He was a betting man and I would often find my way outside the local William Hill in Finsbury Park.

But before he turned into a deadbeat bum, with prostitutes, drink and smoking crack he was an intelligent individual having worked for the British Broadcasting Corporation in some capacity. I have since heard he is dead now passed away with no invitation to the funeral. So, you see how this ended……

It never started…….

I often wonder if she had invested in me, what kind of acting career I would have had but no…..

Yvonne never made it easy

Toy Stories

I started shop lifting at around seven years old for food from the corner shop through sheer destitution, hunger, and survival. On a Sunday I'd run up to Londis on the high road and get us a roast dinner, an oven pie, some tin vegetables, frozen roast potatoes with some Aunt Bessie's Yorkshire puddings. And if it worked out right, I even would manage to get a dessert, apple pie with custard.

Everything non-perishable I stole I kept in my room and accumulated a nice stash. If I needed something that is how I got. I was tired, fed up and was determined to elevate the suffering.

I committed my first burglary when I was still at Junior School I must have been between eight and ten at the time. I roped in some kids from Alma road; my target was St Matthews Primary on South Street. It was during the summer holidays and we broke in but it was so we could colour and draw, we never broke or damaged anything but just played and drawed most of the time we were there.

The thing is Yvonne wasn't one for toys or books; not really, it was my grandmother that taught me how to read, count and do my timetables.

It was my grandmother who would get us black dolls from the USA, nice dresses and treated us like she cared and loved us. She would always let me stay for a night or two when I ran away, having a heart to heart and explaining why I had to go home. It was always temporary with tears when it was time to leave and go back to that hellhole.

Always wanted my own Cindy and Barbie dolls with the clothes and fancy plastic shoes, I was exhausted of second hand shit, and there's no better feeling when unwrapping a new present, a gift, that fresh smell, something mine and new.

My next big plan was to get some new toys, stationary and some smelly erasers. These were rubbers that were in at the time the latest craze, which, looked and smelled like a strawberry, apple, banana and even a hamburger!!!

There was only one place I could get the things I wanted along with some Christmas presents for the family, I know it sounds mad but come Christmas and birthdays we were sometimes kind of like every other family celebrating.

I first saw the big department store "Pearson's" in Enfield town, where I experienced my first burger and fries bought by my older sister's social worker called June, she was real nice. It was opposite the Mac Donald's and sold everything you could think of from furniture, confectionary, clothes, toys, loads and loads of different toys.

I wanted to test my theory initially by myself first and then let the others know but I could not forget entering the store overwhelmed with all the hustle and bustle of shoppers, the bright lights, twinkling of tinsel and the coloured kaleidoscope of Christmas wrapping papers.

I found the toy section and it was busy with nice parents and their children excited about the prospect of what they might find under their Christmas tree if they had been good, and then there was me in the store on my own, having seen the dolls, clothes accessories and stationery I required. It was time to make my next move, I never had any real fear other than Yvonne but even then, I did not care, all the licks and beatings I encountered it never made me a better person in fact I would say it made me mad, detached, angry, resentful and hateful.

"Excuse me madam, Excuse me miss, my mums done some shopping and the bags broke please could I have another carrier bag please?" a quick look I point out to the far end of the store, signalling my mother who is lost amongst the busy shoppers "here you are love take these ". I responded with a smile "thank you" and then I'm gone consumed by the stores bustling waves of Christmas shoppers I head off to fill up my lovely big carrier bags with new goodies.

I went back again this time taking some of the street from Alma road, filling them in on my plan before heading in the store repeating the same scenario this time resulting in a disastrous cost, which I would later come to find out.

I soon learnt that it's not good to have a joint enterprise as someone eventually squealed and I found myself down the cop shop in Enfield town, being seen by a police sergeant. I look back going into his office and not a cell with Yvonne and him agreeing, saying "I never want to see you here again young lady".

And as for all the lovely proceeds of crime I had obtained they were confiscated and thrown in the bin, apart from the purse Yvonne kept and some of the presents I had got for the family.

That night I ran away, jumped out of my top bedroom window into the unknown, lonely and dark night.

I think we both knew that this would not be the last time and Yvonne got used to collecting me from police stations, either as a thief or as a runaway.

Yvonne disappeared for weeks and my best friends mum took us in regularly and we just stayed there and then I just stayed there, until they forced their way in her flat one night and found me hiding. I got a beating that night and was told not to frequent that block or house again. I always went back so appreciative be taken in fed, clothes washed with a longing of normal family life.

In the coming years, I ran away several times with the longest being over three weeks, I ended up in Holloway, Finsbury park with an old male friend of Yvonne's who we had stayed with sometimes in the school holidays. He was a gentle kind old man who was glad for the company with me needing some respite, a person to notice I was gone crying out for help.

But yet, again no one heard me or came to rescue me. The police found me in the end, took me to the station and Yvonne came and picked me up.

I had no voice.

The Colour Purple

Having a Mother who suffered from alcoholism was precarious and a liability, as you were prone to be prey by some very predatory individuals. Most days she would sleep in and not arise until after four or five o clock on a good day, when it was practically finished, regardless of which day of the week it was.

There would be a lot of male traffic but they would come in disguise as friends of the family when in truth some of them were opportunist paedophiles. I do not know if she just didn't care, think or what but in her defence, I would say she was not aware of what was going on.

It was a usual Sunday, Yvonne was upstairs sleeping and me and my sister were playing in the front room. We were both in our night clothes and it must have been around five o clock when we heard the door knock. I couldn't have been more than nine or ten as I was still at Alma Primary School.

Running to the door eager to find out who it was as it might encourage Yvonne to get up, we still hadn't had our dinner yet.

It was a family male friend, who my mother would help out, apparently by reading his post as I think he illiterate and a bit slow.

Shouting, "Mum xxxxx is at the door shall I let him in?" She slowly stirred and groaned "yes". I was always glad for the company it made a change from my sister who was so little at the time. "Hi xxxxx", giving him a big hug and taking his hand to the front room from the passage. He gave me a big hug and a cuddle and asked if Yvonne was coming down? I explained that I tried to wake her and that she had probably fallen back to sleep.

What happened next was a big eye opener and I started to have a suspicious mind from this point onwards at such a young age, but how lucky was I to have sensed where this was going. "Come and sit on my lap?". Thinking nothing of it innocently I did as I was asked to which he responded, "Do you wanna go to the shop and get some sweets? "of course, I'm going to say "Yes Please" he then said "If you take you knickers off, I will give you fifty pence and we can go shop". With that, I recoiled from him and took up my sister who was playing obliviously and we moved to the settee, as far away from him as possible.

I never said another word but my face said it all "you're a bad man". He soon realised this along with the piercing stare I was giving him, he quickly became uncomfortable and left. I remember it like it happened yesterday, things like that never leave you and so I ran upstairs after he left, I truthfully didn't give a fuck if she was upset or not " Mum, Mum xxxxx tried to get in my knickers!!!! ".

I never see Yvonne wake up so rass quick!!! She asked me to repeat everything what had happened and if he had "touched me down below?" relieved I said "No Mum", once she had collected all the necessary information, she then got quickly dressed in a rush, whilst mumbling under her breathe. Once she was ready, she went out, gone for about two hours leaving me with the strictest of instructions not to open the door to anyone from now on.

On her return, she told me she had gone to his house, informed his family what he had done and that he was never to return to the house or go anywhere near any of her kids, and if she ever heard anything like that happen again she would "bore he scunt".

Yvonne was very skilled when it came to a blade or a sharp pair of scissors, she knew exactly how to inflict damage and they were all aware Yvonne had form.

From that day things changed, no male visitors came unannounced or were left alone with us when we were at home and as for xxxxx, he is still alive barely but he makes for a pathetic human being. As far as I am concerned, he is the walking dead, because where he is going if there is an afterlife, a poker, a lot of fire and a chair is waiting with his name on it.

From one risky danger to another and I learnt paedophile's come in many forms even women, but just more subtle.

When Yvonne had a drink binge, which had lasted for a week or so and she was suffering from an episode of depression, she would have a mental breakdown. Smashing up the house screaming, crying and then friends of the family would rally round, advising her to sought help with the drinking. They would come like they were helping but really, it was at a cost to us in the end, we always had to pay one way or another.

We would get clean clothes, food, books and toys to play with in exchange for inappropriate touching at bath time. I recollect it happening once but it was enough for me to know it weren't right.

Basically, we always had to have a bath, when she would "wash us" even though I was big enough to do it myself. I think she got moist by washing down little girls naked bodies with soapy water, and when I did eventually challenge her about it that I could do it myself and clean my sister, she just left. After that weekend, we agreed no matter what happens we ain't going back there again if we can help it. And the days we could not escape we stuck to each other like glue and no door was left unlocked, especially the bathroom.

Just like xxxxx, she knew I knew what she was about and to save her shame made out I was a naughty evil child. Believe it or not, this woman was a devout Christian, Jesus all over the house, this time she's a nonce preying on vulnerable neglected children.

She too is still alive and I just ignore her and cross the street. I don't think her "god" will be very pleased with her "Christian" behaviour; I have to talk the truth "burn bitch burn".

Overall as excruciatingly painful as this all is to relive I still feel I had a miraculous escape, unfortunately, it cannot be said of others……

Grange Hill

I ended up going to Chace Girls School in Enfield, discussed between my big sister and Yvonne they decided that is where I was going without discussion or any opinion on my part considering it was me that was going to be there for the next five years.

Life stayed the same, nothing changed apart from now I'm in secondary school, and I am under pressure to fit in with the popular crowd and keep up with all the latest fashion trends.

It was very hard I had no money, shopping trips for new clothes and that was the least of my problems. I still had the all the others issues going on with food, travel, living expenses and sorting my baby sister.

The day I started my period I told Yvonne and she said "you've turned into a young woman now" and she took me to her room and gave me an old rusty sanitary belt. I was like shit are you fucking kidding me? in my head but vocally explaining, "girls don't use things like that anymore, besides its old I need pads" and with that she reluctantly gave me the money to go shop.

My shopping list began to grow and I bunked off school to go to work instead. Doing some babysitting locally or signing on at a temping agency to work in a factory packing. I needed money and I hated shoplifting.

I missed a lot of school for a variety of reasons and it led back to one person, Yvonne. She would turn up at the school cause a big scene, accusing me of stealing her money. I told the school what was happening at home and they got social services involved.

We were allocated a black social worker who came round to the house and I explained about the food and that our needs were not being met and that she was gambling all the money whilst we were starving. The social worker told me that bingo was Yvonne's one social outlet, so she never heard me and nothing was done.

I decided to sit down with Yvonne and had a conversation about the child benefit, that we needed toiletries and she agreed to give us twenty pounds a month each. This lasted for a short while and then it reverted back to default.

All the older siblings moved out, things were worse than ever, and I tried so hard to attend School, as it was fun, a laugh and a breath of fresh air from the shit that was going on at home. Gradually I became depressed and overwhelmed by all the adversity I was facing and it was becoming increasingly difficult. Yvonne was on benefits so that enabled me to get a free school uniform, school dinners, bus pass, shoes but I was expected to make it last until the next government cheque.

I would leave the house early and meet friends at their house before getting the 191 bus and sometimes I would get a breakfast having woken up, got washed, dressed leaving the house with an empty hungry belly. Some of my friends may have had an idea and would always offer or their parents would make me food.

On the weekends, I did my own shopping going to Enfield town, Wood green, and Holloway road stealing clothes, shoes and the simple things I needed under severe peer pressure. No one wants to hang around with a tramp and whilst no one ever said anything to my face, I know remarks were made about my appearance and my hair. My hair was a big issue for me it being natural, unkempt and hard to manage, I wanted to have it like the rest of my friends straight, flowing and pretty.

I started getting bleaching agents to lighten my skin; if I was a bit fairer maybe I, and people would start to like me.

At fourteen years old, my grandmother died and it broke my heart, to this day, I still miss her so much, with everything that was going on, I was not able to visit and she became sick and less mobile. Due to the funeral I got my hair permed, it was called the wet look but it was high maintenance, costly and short lived.

Out of desperation, I learnt how to braid extensions and at fifteen I decided to relax my hair, I was so happy and felt things were beginning to take a turn for the better in relation to life as a teenager and growing pains.

One evening I came home from school and Yvonne was mad with rage, upset what I had done to my hair and she dragged me upstairs against my will over the bath and proceeded to cut my hair off. I tried to stop her but the damage was done and besides she had control of the scissors. So devastated my hair chopped in all different lengths I had no other choice but to go back to plait extensions.

My skin was messed up due to the Hydroquinone having an adverse effect, stress and the unbalanced diet. My life was in disarray, nothing was working out no matter how hard I tried and this woman was driving me literally to suicide.

I used Weed, Marathons, Thunder Bird and Canie to anaesthetise the pain on occasions but it was not around for long, that feeling of euphoria would dissipate and all the old wounds and reality would be back, resurfacing, haunting me again.

One morning I could not face going to school so I bought a draw, walked to the big Tesco's, built a big fat zoot and waited for the 121 bus. On the empty bus I blazed my spliff with the windows open to aerate the smell and off I went buzzing out my tree but this draw was different, comatose unable to move drifting off high…high…high….

I stayed on till the last stop and then took the same bus back. Later on I made some enquiries "what the fuck was I smoking?" "Skag Ash" heroin and hashish resin mixed together and I was like "oh ok" in my mind I made a concrete decision I am going to make sure I never purchase that shit again and I didn't.

School was no longer an interest, I had missed too much and my friends had moved on, boyfriends, studying and social events. Even the school weren't bothered anymore I came in and left when I wanted and nothing was said.

I could not control what was happening but I could control my body it was malnourished anyway so I just stopped eating and became anorexic. Yvonne never noticed but my older sister did, seeing I was only eating biscuits and drinking tea. She would visit and entice me by cooking my favourite meal spaghetti Bolognese.

I became very withdrawn, self-harming and extremely obsessed with washing my hands and O.C.D, avoidance paranoia of touching dirty doorknobs.

With the lack of food, just the biscuits and hot drinks I would involuntarily gag and puke infrequently. Yvonne got it wrong and thought I was pregnant, battering me in the front room, shouting and demanding answers. I had none for her and I just could not be arsed, I did not run or defend myself I let her get on with it and when she was finished, I went to my room.

My sixteenth birthday came and Yvonne treated it like it was any other normal day. My brother's wife at the time got me a card, present and celebratory drinks to celebrate. In the evening I came back and said "Yvonne it's my birthday, I'm sixteen" unemotionally she retorted, "so what, what do you want me to do about it? I stayed at my sister in laws that night and got very drunk indeed.

I lost the will to live and I tried to kill myself again, for the second time with tablets from the kitchen cupboard. Again, I woke up and I was pissed off, don't know what I took it was a prescribed medication and I swallowed about thirty tablets.

It never worked and I felt awful, high temperature, shivers along with diarrhoea. As I lay in bed still hoping theirs a chance, I kept asking god why he keeps letting me live.

Back to School
(Enfield College)

I was still resolute that I could turn things around and decided to go to college and become a social worker instead, a decent social worker, a person of care. All my dreams of becoming an Actress dissolved, faded becoming a memory of the past and unachievable.

Enfield College did not want me due to my disruptive, challenging and rebellious nature towards authority and I had several interviews both by myself and with Yvonne.

I got in eventually and managed to get a grant, with plenty of support both financially and personally.

The home life was still the same but there was still a glimmer of hope for me. I always knew the life I had been given was the wrong one and it had now become my crusade.

The grant I got from the borough council went into Yvonne's bank account and at the start; I was getting an allowance every week to cover college. I really did like college especially the common room we would get nuff jokes, black jack, chess, pool and of course gossip.

At the time it was all about this girl, we know that had just had a baby, which she sometimes brought to college, and my little sister later went on to have a baby at approximately aged fifteen. There was no chance of that happening to me I was a tomboy and moved with dah man dem, they all loved me but only like a sister.

Part of my course modules was to go on a work experience residential in a care-setting environment. We were told it was at the "Winged Fellowship" based at Redhill in Surrey, a respite facility for children and their carer's.

I always roped in my big sister and she has been my rock, with me, helped, and supported. I was very apprehensive about going to this place because it was way out of London, probably no black people and I had to share a room.

Having spoken to the course manager, I negotiated my sister coming to help out as a volunteer and be a positive mentor for the group of teenagers. We got there by coach and we had been duped, there we no bloody kids, it was for disabled adults and older people.

Our accommodation was outside of the main residential care home and backed off behind it was a massive forest, half a fence and then our wooden bungalow. There were no locks on any of the doors and that threatened my personal space, privacy and safety.

I shared a room with my sister who arranged a meeting with us as a group resigned, decided to stay and give our time. Either the home was understaffed or we had been well and truly shafted, prepared for our arrival in relation to cutting costs. We were assigned to look after residents in twos but that was not always feasible. They were wheeled out early after breakfast into the garden and left, if it was not for us they would be no communication until lunch.

In the afternoon, a coach would arrive and take them out for the day before returning for evening tea. I fucking hated it and I voiced that they were taking the piss, exploiting us and in retaliation, they disliked me.

There was some shagging going on with some of the girls from my class and members of male staff. It was so annoying as the girls got up at five in the morning, used all the hot water and were made up ready for the day.

We were doing toilets runs, bathing, hoisting, dressing and undress, feeding, colostomy bags, catheters and enema's.

I chuckle about it now but at the time I truly felt like what we were being subjected to was horrific and a form of abuse. We had not been given no form of adequate training and I witnessed some incidents, including the first time I seen projectile excrement. That evening we all got stoned and had a laugh about what we had experienced.

Back in London same old same and I had assignments to do with deadlines to complete. However, with the situation on going, it became impossible. Started missing days and surviving everyday became my priority.

Those that did help when they could by giving us food and money for electric became naturally resentful and therefore I decided to no longer ask for assistance.

Yvonne was not even leaving the money now like she used to before, I eventually found out she spent it all on bingo.

The college tried and so did I and I tried again and failed again this time at Muswell Hill College.

And the same thing happened, I felt trapped and thoughts of me having to leave enters my mind…..

Nightmare on South Street

There were numerous deaths in the area from the tramp found dead on South Street to drug addicts, passed away in the derelict garages where we used to play.

We also had suicide jumpers from the huge tower blocks, my best friend who was run over by a van and died straight in front of me, and another dear play friend who drowned after playing on the ice in the River Lee.

I swear this place was plagued with tragedy too many people lost their life's from neighbours and friends in car crashes, to jealousy, murder and revenge.

It was a typical Saturday and I remember a sports programme being on the television when there was a knock at the door.

"It's the police can we come in please". Two tall officers came into the living room where I was sitting and one of them told Yvonne to send me upstairs. I knew it was serious from one being plain clothed, I figured he was a detective on the case and I did as I was directed, spying from the top of the stairs into the room trying to listen but all I could hear was murmurs and that there had been an incident with one of my brothers.

Yvonne was escorted to the police station and we were sent to a neighbour's in the block. That evening I found out that my brother had killed someone apparently, an ongoing feud ignited by a girl and included others who instigated the beef.

As I think back my older brother was an outsider and new to the area. He was a stranger even to me and I was adjusting to having a new older brother who I thought was really cool. He was a fantastic dancer, roller skater but he was showy and flash with it and I think that pissed certain people right off.

I had a keen interest in dance from a young age and I have been told by family members that I would be put out to dance in the pubs and Yvonne would collect the money. Years later my brother taught me some moves, routines and I entered a few competitions and won but I never took it any further.

My brother was sociable like the rest of the older siblings, ingratiating with the young people and his fair share of the women on the street. This ruffled many feathers and put noses out of joint that certain individuals colluded to plan for his demise.

It was a weeknight and I heard loud banging from the front door, I opened the door after him shouting for help. As I opened it, he swiftly barged his way into the front room and then I noticed he was injured as if he had been in a fight. There was blood and he was slanted in his stature so I'm guessing he had probably dislocated his shoulder and broken his hand. Yvonne came back and the house filled quickly with bodies dissecting what had transpired that evening at the local youth centre. Everyone thought mistakenly that it would pass and fade but we all were unaware that it this was to be the beginning of a series of catastrophic incidents, which would eventually lead to death.

We started getting funny phone calls, knocks on the door and I began to feel scared. No one was telling me what was going on apart from the odd overheard conversations I was snatching.

The night of the fight, it was supposedly sorted with a gentleman's handshake with the understanding that the conflict between both men had been extinguished.

My Brother some felt he did not belong, having not grown up in the manner people became narked but were like smiling assassins and he was never genuinely accepted as "one of us".

The situation escalated with unconfirmed tales, spreading everywhere in a frenzied contagion of bubbling pandemonium.

The next violent exchange was at a snooker tournament based within the local youth club where my brother nearly lost his life. His throat was slashed in a strategic organised operation with the sole intention of causing death. The blade missed 2 millimetres from his jugular vein and the Dr told him any deeper he would have died.

The perpetrator got 28 days jail and then he was released and the cycle carried on, it had become like an obsession and people were feeding both their egos, and pride along with the tyranny of mischief.

The day my brother killed, He was on the bus and they happened to meet up, this I find unbelievably remarkable that this was not orchestrated on purpose. The fight moved from off the bus to the high road, where the victim was stabbed and lost his life.

Then we were all targets feeling unsafe, the media had him plastered over the papers and I was having to still go school with all the pointing of fingers and swirling misinformation that was going around the school.

We also had the lovely neighbours who Yvonne confided in at that dark time only for them to have regurgitated the private information to others in the neighbourhood.

I will never forget the night I saw the victim's brother staring at us from across the road, he was standing outside the school, he had been crying, his tears glistening against the evening street lights. He was older than I was and his attire was a secondary school type of uniform. I wanted to apologise as I looked in his face I saw his pain and grief we had both lost people we cared about and for what?

The death contributed to the passing of my grandmother and it was dreadful especially when my brother turned up outside the Enfield

Crematorium, which was littered with beautiful colourful wreaths, and then him handcuffed with guards in tow. It's so mournful as her ashes were sent back to Guyana where she could be with her mother. It was and still is one of the darkest days in my life amongst many and I miss her terribly, with every Mother's Day being so bleak as I recall crying during the funeral service, wishing it was Yvonne that had died instead and let my nan live.

Years later the murder would come back to haunt me in my teenage years calling me "black rat "and then mention whose sister I was. Sometimes I tried to deny it, because it had nothing do with me but I still got the negative ripple effect.

What is even more strange is that years later a similar death would soon repeat itself.

There was a social club called the "Tenants Association", which was a place where everyone hung out, day trips, bingo and disco's. Occasionally there was a wedding or party from one of the locals, it was the place to be.

Loads of things happened; there were fights, affairs, drug dealing and a lot more. I recall one evening I had escaped from the house by going to the shop for tobacco for Yvonne and ended up there, it was a place to catch up on gossip, check friends and was a lively social hub when used positively.

Well I must have lost track of time talking with friends, when I felt some blows come from behind, it was Yvonne striking me publically with a fucking tree branch!!! How fucking shameful and so embarrassing, as I fled from the mad woman and the tree branch in shock, I began to seriously think what the hell is wrong with this witch.

I recollect another time a member brought his dog in, it was around the early time staffs and American pit bulls has just became known and this dog went berserk, we were jumping on table and chairs as the dog went uncontrollably crazy, I think it may of bit a few people and was eventually put down.

It all went a bit tits up when gangs of youths from different areas starting attending, intimidating the local guys. The youths were from up the road and further, the first time I clapped eyes on them was on the 191 bus from Enfield town after school. They proceeded to strip the bus on the top deck awash with school kids and rob them of their valuables, which included jewellery, money, watches and anything else, which took their fancy.

The bus driver was too frightened and played dumb whilst we were in fear subjected to possible violence if you did not play ball. Lucky I was ok with my broke ass so I never got robbed but I did get abuse about my how dark and ugly I was, but it never bothered me much just now and then.

They even had young impressionable vulnerable girls from my school in such trepidation that they would shoplift to order mainly clothes from stores in Enfield and Edmonton.

The youths started attending the tenant's association club and hanging around the area, which was an absolute travesty considering what occurred in the coming months.

With the influx of diversity, some white folk became unhappy and moved further afield otherwise known as white flight to Hertford, Cheshunt and the surrounding areas.

I did try to encourage Yvonne to move to Tottenham, which she did consider for a while, but others in the family decided it was not a good idea so we stayed in ponders end much to my annoyance.

All I remember was seeing a pair of trainers and a body covered in a blanket outside one of the tower blocks. He had been stabbed; it was one of the youths not from the area, who had apparently robbed a local of some jewellery, which resulted in his death.

It was such a sorrowful time another young life lost and for what? Two families lives shattered, friends broken and hearts distressed. Shortly after the tenant's association club closed suddenly, whispers about dodgy money and financial inaccuracies.

Alma road was never the same again.

What's Love Got To Do With It

The first time I met the then love of my life I was eleven years old and had no idea in years to come he would become the father of my child and that I would experience so much pain.

After my visit to the police station and the stern talking to regarding the crimes I had committed Yvonne decided that myself and baby sister would spend the next six weeks summer holiday away from Alma road, so we went to Finsbury park and stayed with her friend and kids. Little did she know that she had placed us out of the frying pan into the fire, as well putting us, our safety at risk again.

Yvonne's friend was a bingo goer, mate and her kids were going through chaos just like us but it was on a different scale. We stayed with three siblings a son who was the eldest and two daughters, one pregnant and the other who was a tomboy. Initially we thought it was fun a new area, and making friends but we soon came to see the bullying, violence, and drug dealing. It was whilst I was here I met my future baby father, we got on and I fancied him but he was never interested in me.

I regretfully experienced shop lifting again, some drug dealing and my baby sister receiving unwanted advances from dirty old black men.

We tried to keep in contact and years later when I was seventeen I decided to return and catch up on how they was doing. It was good seeing everyone, we reminisced at our younger experiences together, and they welcomed me with open arms that I decided to stay the night.

Approximately about 6 o clock in the morning I heard some stones being thrown at the window and it turned out to be him, he was so tall and handsome I fell immediately back in love, he was beautiful and I weren't so ugly now, I dressed like a girl now and had all the bumps and shapes in the right places.

That day we got on so well, discussed how we had changed so much and we flirted together expressing our liking for each other. That same day he came back staying with me in Enfield. Talking and laughing into the late hours grateful, he was with me as I came back to a lonely empty house.

I was so naive having had not many boyfriends, wanting so much for someone to take an interest and care for me, he did that but it came with consequences.

I smile wryly as I remember when we consummated our relationship, and the next day we went to the phone box together where he ended it with his then girlfriend. I felt so special he was serious about me.

Yvonne came back and was horrified when she realised who he was, she hated him with a vengeance finding every opportunity to tell me how he was no good and a bad seed. Thinking back, she was probably right but who was she to talk not as if I had a good template to work from?

He came from a troubled life growing up and we understood each other, the more Yvonne cursed, and denigrated our relationship the more stronger it grew, and we became close. He was real telling me how awful Yvonne was, my treatment and that I was like a Cinderella. He opened my eyes to so many things and strangely empowered me.

Yvonne was not happy with the relationship and banned him staying, but it was cool we pre-planned together; we pretended he was coming to visit daily and he would come and wait outside in the late hours of the morning, climbing up through my bedroom window. So romantic as I vision us as a ghetto Romeo and Juliet against all odds our loved prevailed. I would sneak him into my room and there was this one time Yvonne had a suspicion and burst into my room looking around expecting me to be caught out, the room was empty so she thought but he was hiding under my bed with his big size tens hanging out under the bottom. Luckily, she never noticed and we joked together quietly late into the night.

I had witnessed violence growing up but my first own experience was with him. I recall him having wrapped his big hands around my neck strangling me after an argument about an ex-girlfriend he was goading me with and so I broke the necklace she had bought. My little sister stormed in and preceded to fight him, I intervened to me it had just gotten all out of hand explaining to my sister she had nothing to worry about.

He apologised emphatically and we moved on I thought his behaviour was because he really cared, he had issues, we both did I suppose that was the bind that kept us together but I knew he cared for me. We were intimate for about six months of our relationship in the dark, me taking off all my clothes under the duvet cover, him never seeing my naked body, being patient, gentle, and kind until he thought I was ready.

Yvonne eventually forbid him from coming over to the point in the end Yvonne detested him so much she gave me an ultimatum, leave him and stay or be with him and go.

He had enlightened me to so much, wise about life and was a positive in my life at that time, excluding the first fight he was my everything and so I left, heading to postcode N4, Finsbury Park. My life in his hands I trusted him and this was to be a new start. To my horror, his place was worse than mine, junk everywhere and no food, seriously at Alma road at least we had biscuits this was real poverty.

It was horrendous nothing to eat or drink, we turned into Bonnie and Clyde but I was shit. He never got me involved and I would stand watch at the end of the road whilst he robbed innocent male passer bys, who were either coming home from work maybe or visiting a girlfriend or family member.

It was appalling but we were fed and I think he began to like it and I no longer came out, him returning with food, jewellery, jackets and stuff.

Once changed he tried to dominate and control me with violence I always fought back, but it was usually a slap, or throttled with a spew of verbal abuse. I certainly began to miss home after a fight where I ran out the flat and he left me outside in the cold all night.

On my return things had changed in such a short space of time, my sister had moved into my room and Yvonne purred like the cat who had got the cream.

The demand still stood, leave him and come back, he was afflicted, I still loved him and would never leave so I took a bag of clothes and returned to N4.

I got used to the physical fighting and the mental abuse but he was always loving and sorry after and I became conditioned to the domestic violence.

After a while then it began to take its toll and the hunger got to me. Emotionally he broke me down and I became a shadow of my former self no longer fierce and strong but weak, broken and sad.

Later I moved into my older sisters flat with him by my side to Stamford hill, where she pulled a few strings and eventually got me a hostel in

White Hart lane. She liked my boyfriend at first but she soon came to dislike him due to his treatment of me.

Once in the hostel things got worse the violence just weren't physical it began to include knifes, stabbing, slices, and I made it worse by fighting back. I always relate our relationship to some Ike and Tina turner shit, it went deep and I always stayed.

Jealousy and unfaithfulness began to infect our fucked up relationship, he controlled seeing my friends, when I could go out even locking me in my own room and the one time I managed to escape, him having confiscated all my shoes I ran out in his size ten trainers, running for help down Northumberland park road entering a newsagent telling them of my impending danger and them responding "sorry I'm not getting involved". By the time, I found a phone box he was already waiting for me, shaking his head in disappointment marching me back to the Hostel.

The dysfunction love cycle continued and I became pregnant, unemployed, no career my worst nightmare. He was over the moon at the start berating me at the thought of me having a termination.

The voice of reason was telling me this was not ideal for us to raise a child, we had nothing to offer and I was nineteen at college studying.

I remember the night our son was conceived it was in love, persuaded by him and my best friend I never made it to the abortion clinic. Once pregnant I got most of the support from family and friends with him becoming quite distant as my body changed.

Inevitably, I found out he had been unfaithful, heart broken and distressed after a fight, where he punched me in my pregnant state. Feeling alone and of no self-worth I tried to kill myself again for the third time. Rushed to north Middlesex hospital and had my stomach pumped, thankfully glad the baby and me were safe.

I returned to the hostel and called a women's refuge and by the next afternoon, I was moved out. Stuck in a dingy refuge based in Waltham cross, riddled with mice unloved and isolated I began to miss him.

Like a bounty hunter, he tracked me down and I kinda liked the fact he was looking for me. It was twisted but I knew he did love me and that is why I kept on going back to him.

Got thrown out the refuge when I took him back disgusted with me I let myself down but I had a baby to think about and I did not want to be a single parent I wanted better for this little one.

Our son was born after I lost copious amounts of blood requiring a transfusion as well as a caesarean, he never made it to the birth with me and I held on for 16 hours waiting for him.

A few months later after the hate had departed on my part he did really try to be the best father he could be but in truth he weren't ready and the volatile abuse continued along with the infidelity, shit he weren't even hiding it no more.

I had enough and it came to blows fighting in my one room hostel in Palmers green, my son on the bed my only witness watching as his father stabbed me in the thigh so relentlessly that the knife entered through one side and exited on the other.

I was in crutches for weeks with the police looking for him to press charges, as he ran away not taking his responsibility like a man.

During this time, I got my flat in Edmonton, N9 and I was hoping for a fresh new start but not as a single parent I had experienced that and its not nice and I definitely never wanted it for my son so I took him back again.

The police were incandescent with sadness when I said, "sorry I want to drop the charges please". He was certainly on route to HMP and I would never have been able to live with myself telling my son why I shopped his dad to jail.

We started again and things were good for a while I got a job went back to college and he did nothing not even look after his own son.

I soon realised he was a token dad present in name only but never done shit, we did get engaged but the arguing and outside interference contributed to the breakdown off the relationship. His mother returned from abroad and she never liked me. I put off going to university and I began to see him for what he was especially after he wanted me to have another baby and beat me because I purchased myself a brand new mobile phone with my own hard earned money.

I stayed with him for six years in total and I really did try to make it work, I am not a quitter but fuck me I should have let it go a long time ago.

He left having irregular contact with his son, not being a proper father. My son is a grown man now but he needed his father and I did the best I could by him. He let his son down badly but am so lucky to have known my Son's grandad who actively made up for his son's lack of involvement. God rest his soul he passed away from cancer.

R.I.P David XxX

Bugs Bunny to Beauty Queen

When I told him the relationship was finished we were both looking out at the big windows facing the Edmonton green roundabout. He never flinched or tried to fight it was as if he was happy it was finally over, relieved.

It was hard for my son as he missed his dad and me too after a while, an empty bed. I got on with work but the red wine became my best friend and I even tried to get him back but alas, it was too late fortunately for me.

I threw myself into my job, college and for relief I would attend the local pub on an evening and weekend with my son, who loved pool and played very well.

I felt freedom dressing nice and taking pride in my appearance something I never had the chance to do when I was with my son's dad and oh did I start to cause some traffic. Then I started raving with a bad crew but I had mad fun until I weren't making it to work, raving from Friday till Monday, fucked. All the new male attention had me gassed, I ain't gonna lie after being told I'm ugly, useless and no one don't want a baby mother.

It was really a new start and I flourished. I started dating and had a few relationships but they never lasted.

Sometimes it was because I had a child or they lost interest when I told them about my aspirations to be an Actress, initially impressed but then later when the excitement had worn off laughing in amusement, telling me to get a proper job.

Then I decided that I would no longer get involved in relationships as my last partner turned out to be a nightmare who was controlling, verbally abusive and ended up stalking me when I finished it for approximately two years. Maybe it was my fault too not wanting to be tied down or choosing the wrong boyfriends who already had their partners and would never leave them.

My Son was always looked as best as I could and I made sure he was self-sufficient, can use the washing machine, cook and had general awareness. He was independent having to go school on his own using the bus with me being a single parent going to work.

My baby father tried to bun (hurt) me weeks later turning up in my local pub with his chick in a public display of affection to try and hurt me but I was like raggo (I don't care) poor bitch. Years later my son's dad did apologise for the way he treated me.

I decided I was tired of the same old jobs, I was not happy and nor was the employer with me rocking up late sometimes still drunk and no interest in doing the job I was employed to do. My mother never really told me what to do so it was a bit hard to conform; I was a rebel before you know it gross misconduct. However, it was cool Ms Janet and I fronted it out, I won and we came to an arrangement. They told me I was better than this, or they just wanted rid but I have a great respect for them either way they believed in my aspirations and gave me time off when I got my first acting job, the whole office loved it and I thanked them all.

A photographer contacted me later that same year explaining he would like to do a few test shots, he remarked that I had nice features and could do modelling.

Personally, I was astounded me a model, I don't think so.

I'm Coming Out

From then on I was on a mission, even got sponsorship, thank you Elizabeth I was serious about this. I signed with several acting agencies, enrolled on an evening and weekend course. If I had any chance of having a career, I would have to put in some effort. It was important for me to know what happens behind the scenes as well as in front of the camera. Then the work started rolling in from corporate roleplays to stage work, modelling, television and film.

There was a lot of pitfalls along the way, dodgy agents, casting couch directors, numerous rogue agencies and I did get duped a fair few times but it never deterred me and the rewards far outweighed the bad so I kept it moving.

Rejection has been a big part of my life so it only makes sense in a peculiar way to want to be in the hardest industry in the world where it is part of the journey.

My first acting job was James Bond "Die another Day" with Pierce Brosnan. I only had a small part as a Cuban cigar roller in a factory.

Proper excited having had my costume fitting in the renowned costumiers Angels based in Hendon.

I had to wear an awfully loud in colour all in one cat suit but I did not care. It was a great opportunity to see how the film industry works, how actresses behave, and what a long day it can be working on a set. Another reason why I am proud of this achievement as this is the last film Pierce Brosnan played Bond. He is a quaint, down to earth human being who took time to speak with us and sign autographs; I did not ask, as I never get star struck, they are normal people who just happen to work in the film and TV business.

Then I got parts on ITV's Bad Girls as nurse Anne Black, a secretary on BBC one's Panorama programme, which was an interesting documentary about the death of government scientist Dr David Kelly.

I got some modelling jobs and television commercials, even booked for a corporate training DVD for British airways where I played an unruly drunk passenger. I enjoyed being a jobbing actor testing my commitment to the craft by going on tour for three months to Newcastle, where there was no diversity; people embraced me like an alien and a kid no more than five years old called me a "paki".

Although subjected to many challenges whilst away from home I made the sacrifices knowing I could handle this journey, the treacherous people contaminating the industry and exploiting the young and naïve hungry to make it.

Sometimes when you are so driven with the one thing on your mind every day striving eagerly in order to get closer to the goal, you can lose sight of common sense. Especially when a lot of the work you do can be low paid, when a lot of the castings are for Caucasian actresses and in an industry where the market is so oversubscribed, it can seem heaven sent when the ideal job comes along with a great performance fee and a fabulous opportunity or so I thought. But it was in fact a dangerous scam that I had applied for on Gumtree.

I have not talked about this incident until now but I think it is necessary so that it does not happen to anyone else also. At the time, I was so embarrassed and ashamed but now I am about raising awareness.

What I did not know was the casting was fake, the producer & director was fake and I was on my way to audition for an insidious pervert who lured me knowing that he sexually assaulted me.

If it's too good to be true it's probably not and I found out the hard way but I am blessed that I am alive to tell the tell as it could of played out so differently as you will find out in the next chapter…..

Panic Room

I was doing my usual daily routine of job searching online, checking the regular acting sites for work. In the past I had place ads on gumtree and applied also successfully gaining employment so when I saw the advertisement "TV producers seeks black actress for television pilot" I responded initially sending over my photograph and C.V. Within a few hours, I had received a response back with me asking for more information about the show and pay.

He explained that it was a thriller pilot for ITV detailing all the information I required including the pay per episode which was reasonable to be fair. We had communicated with several emails prior to him inviting me to audition.

He gave me the time and address of where the audition was taking place giving me his number in case I got lost.

Initially my little sister was due to come with me but she couldn't make it so I text her the details, when I was leaving, when I arrived that's how do I things in order to keep myself safe.

Jumped on the bus on route not having a clue but I was safe and my sister had all the details should anything untoward happen.

I text him explaining where I was and he told me where to get off and that he would come and collect me, which is nothing unusual again in the industry with a runner coming to meet you, before meeting the director and auditioning.

He came to collect me, telling me more about the project, the character and what he was looking for which seemed natural. We arrived in a private road Cul De Sac and I remember a neighbour mentioning how busy it was with all the ladies, so the neighbour obviously knew him and I didn't think nothing of it as I entered the house I looked all around, there were family pictures around of a wife and kids which I assumed were his when I questioned him on their whereabouts he told me they had gone on holiday and he had to stay behind due to filming.

We went into the open kitchen area where I was able to read the synopsis and prepare the lines required of me, taking direction in order to make the scene.

At the start I had to film stating my name and the project, and for fake scene I had to hide and crawl on the floor in a scared hostage situation, we went through the scene several times and then him finally filming the scene.

He was calm throughout, discussing his previous work as I followed him upstairs to do the last part of the audition, which was a bedroom scene. He explained that it was me, my boyfriend in bed and that I had to be topless. I asked where the other actor was and he said it was a small part and that he had not cast for him yet, that he would stand in for him.

He left the room so I can take off my top half or so I thought which I did and jumped in the bed as he came in stating we would have to simulate being a couple. It was here he sexually abused me trying to force kiss, touching and kissing my breasts. Thinking in my mind this shit needs to be over quick but actors have these uncomfortable scenes at some stage, that I'd already played a lesbian kissing murderer on stage, and it did not mean anything to me, it was the character. In all it must have lasted approximately three minutes and when it was over he left the room again so I could get dressed. It was whilst I was getting ready to leave that my sister text me and me telling him on his return that for safety I had given all his information to her and she was just checking that I was alright. Seriously, I think that text may have saved my life and he let me go.

 I did feel highly uncomfortable and awkward afterwards as we left, him returning me the bus stop telling me I should hear from him in the next few days.

As I sat on the bus, recollecting all of what had transpired I began to think things just weren't right. Later on, that same evening I had overheard some other black actors' had applied to the casting with some having left finding him dodgy and refusing to do the bedroom scene. I decided to forget about it and move on if he had lured me there on false pretences karma will surely get him. I felt so stupid like I should of seen it but it was only in hindsight I realised.

Weeks had passed I never heard nothing back and I was on another acting job when I received a called from a private number "Can I speak to Sharron please?

It was a woman her voice was serious, responding cautiously "speaking". She went on "you attended an audition which was filmed where he touched you and several other girls inappropriately. We have confiscated some of his laptops, phone and video recorder whilst we investigate and trace the other women on the recordings.

I was in fucking shock as I braced against the wall and steps at London bridge station, it was rush hour but it became silence all the commuters blocked out hustling to get home but just the quiet of me and this copper on the phone. "We would like you to come down to the station and make a statement please?"

Still in shock and more embarrassed about who else in the police force had seen the footage, my 34b's and the assault. With this all in mind I declined saying I couldn't help especially if it went to court, I could not be associated with it. Imagine if my name became famous for an assault and not for my talents as an actress or writer, maybe the industry blaming me saying it is my own fault and me blacklisted never to work again, fuck that.

Rushing home I felt so angry having realised that it was all false there was never going to be no pilot, I had been taken for a fool and assaulted as well.

As soon as I got back, I traced his email address and sent him an angry email about what he had done to me, the police phone call, gloatingly informing him that he was in big trouble. He emailed me back denying any, such thing had happened and that it was all untrue.

Whilst I did not get involved in the legal process, he was eventually charged and arrested. If it went to court or not I never did find out but thankfully, I am still here to tell my experience and inform young girls to be careful. There are some unscrupulous people out there male and female who prey on ambitious actors trying to work and gain a respectable name. Accruing a decent pedigree of work with the hope, that next job could potentially make them into a household star or lead to that big opportunity you have been working towards.

Please do your research, check their previous work history, google search their name see what comes up. Share the meeting time and place with a close family member. Always meet in a public place and if you can bring a friend with you.

Real producers and directors never do filming alone and will always have a third person or more present. Any intimate scenes are disclosed immediately, discussed in length and you not expected to perform naked, or topless at the audition process.

Touched by Angels

The last official date I went on was Saturday 6th August 2011. Two days prior to me going on that date a young black man had been shot dead by the police in the borough of Tottenham. I had been following it closely on sky news and had seen the small demonstration on the local street, the community wanted answers from the police and the police were trying to work as if it was just another day in the office, when they had taken another black life.

I was meeting my date in the heart of Covent Garden in a nice brassiere bar and was looking forward to some male company as a friend or maybe possibly something more if the friendship progressed and I liked him. I had been single for time and it would be nice to grow old with a loving partner and share things together.

Got onto the overhead train and was alarmed when the trained stopped and I saw people running up and down in the road on Bruce Grove high street. This is where I should of jumped on to the opposite side of the station and gone home but I chose to carry on, thinking it will have all calmed down by the time I return home.

Met with my date in central London the city was busy as usual nothing untoward, and he seemed quite pleasant. We had a few drinks and then he suggested we move on to a club called EGG London.

We got in a cab and we headed to the club, he asked me to pay the cab and we went inside and it was packed. I had my time of raving but I had not been out in ages and the scene was different. My date gave me a drink and then soon disappeared leaving me dazed, alone and scared in a full nightclub.

I tried to look for him but it was impossible so I decided to leave hopefully I would bump into him outside.

Staggering to the cash point to see if I had any money to get home, it was empty as I came to the realisation disorientated that I had been drugged and left stranded outside a nightclub I began to cry on the side of the road.

Partygoers and security did not question why I was alone or upset; just assuming I was a drunk left behind from her group of friends. My mascara and make up had run and became smudged I was now a mess having worn that evening a nice dress quite short and extremely high heels with a clutch bag. My phone was dead and I was at a total loss, what dah fuck was I gonna do?

I must have been a crying loudly as two people came over to me concerned and asked me what had happened.

I told them; shocked they offered to sort out a cab for me but they were on their way home after all it was late. They explained that they were genuine I could have been their sister or niece, assuring me that they would get me home. Looking into both these white's men's eyes I genuinely trusted them and left.

One of the gentlemen lived around the corner from Amy Winehouse in a converted warehouse, he was an artist, and the other male was his best friend.

The owner gave a single room downstairs with a bed and blanket, told me to rest, and discuss about getting me home tomorrow.

It was the early afternoon when I finally woke up and ran upstairs to charge my phone and thank them both for the kindness they had shown a complete stranger. The warehouse was set on three floors and was very nice with his media and artwork displayed throughout the property.

They made me fried breakfast and they confirmed that I had definitely been spiked due to my behaviour. I tried to call that punk to let him know what had happened to me but his phone was switched off.

I thanked them immensely calling them my two white angels as we laughed about it, they both stressed that they could not of left me in that state.

I found out his best friend lived hedonistically on a barge by the river it was him that called the cab for me to get home, however there was a big problem no cabs were going past seven sisters due to the riots, fires and looting which had taken place the night before. We eventually managed to get a cab that was willing to risk taking me home back to Enfield. As we exchanged numbers, I promised I would call to pay back the taxi fare and take them for a drink as I gladly climbed in the cab, and waved goodbye again I thanked god for sending them to look after me.

It took me ages to get home and seven sisters was cordoned off just before the police station was and the burnt skeletal remnants of a big red bus. We turned right onto the new road and I was so glad to be home, jumped in the bath and caught up with all the madness of the riots with events spreading to Enfield town, my ends and further afield even to obscure places like West Bromwich, Battersea and Bristol.

And the angels, a few weeks later I made contact with one of them, he was well and did not want any of the money back.

We arranged to meet up for a drink but the plans fell through and we lost touch.

As for my date, he rang up about two days later asking if I was ok by voicemail of course as I never spoke to him again, removing him from all my social media and vowing to myself no more dating it's not for me.

Family Talk

When I decided to write this book about my life, what was fundamentally important to me is that it is factual, truthful, honest and fair.

In this chapter, you will hear my sister's, Lissette Pillay's account of her own childhood to adult journey, which is different to mine but has similar strands running throughout....

"I was born in 1966, being the middle child of five children by Yvonne Pillay. I know my mother was pregnant with me whilst serving a sentence at Holloway prison but I was not aware, I was born inside prison until later on. I spent the first eighteen months in HMP Holloway with my mother due to the fact my father's family did not want me, only my brother. Once the time came I could no longer stay with mum, they took me in reluctantly living with my brother.

From the age of approximately three or four until I was seventeen, I had been in out of the care system. At around the age of six, Sharron's father came to take her away for the weekend and failed to return so my mother decided to go and look for her. She was gone for about three weeks, leaving myself and my two older siblings to fend for ourselves. Whilst mum was away, someone contacted social services and we were taken into care, with the eldest going to live with his father.

My first recollection of being in residential care was when I was eleven with my brother, we was sent to Tankerton, Whitstable based in Kent, initially it was to be for a short stay as the matter was going through the legal process, mum had been charged.

The Salvation Army ran the care home, I remember vividly having to call the staff major, captain, and brigadier at all times.

They did not try to or know how to cater for black skin or hair, as there were only three black people in total at the residence.

My grandmother (mum never came to see us) would visit us and bring West Indian food, however after she left, the staff would spray air-freshener throughout the property.

My brother and I were very close and I think that is due to the fact we are from the same dad, and ours was the only one she married.

I was the only girl for eight years and felt isolated and lonely as I did all the washing, dragging it to the laundry, and the cooking.

Later on in life, my mother told me she never wanted any girls, she always wanted boys and my Nan caught her in the toilet trying to get rid of me, with a knitting needle.

She kept me in the end because of my grandmother. Mum had eleven pregnancies' but only five children, whether they were miscarriages, still born or abortions only she and god knows.

Mum gave them life but I nurtured them without me they would not be here as mum was an alcoholic and there was no dad about.

The Break Spears Arm pub was a place mum frequented all the time.

I would have a glass of Coke with the straw and a packet of Golden Wonder. My mum would bring me and my baby sister Sharron, who would dance and customers would throw money at her, which my mum would collect and put towards more alcohol. Mum came home often with different men and I remember waking up in the morning with strange men in the house.

On one occasion, I did mention to my mother that one of her male friends was looking at me, making me feel very uncomfortable. She did not take my concerns seriously and some months later, I was abused.

After the incident, my brother whom I am very close to knew something was wrong with me and asked me what was wrong and I said nothing. When I finally told him after many years had past, he was very angry and upset, as he knew something had happened.

I do remember when my sister Sharron was born, I was so happy it was like having my own little dolly, I also recall having to get up feed and change her as my mum was always drunk. I used to go into my mother's room and purposely wake Sharron up by pinching her just so I could have some company.

Which is funny because years later when I had my own daughter, Sharron would do the exactly the same.

From a young age I kept the house by doing shopping, laundry either by hand over the bath or taking black sacks to the local launderette, cooking, plaiting hair and making sure the older siblings school uniform was ready which included mine and my two brothers. I also had to do my mothers and the babies clothes and press them with no iron. In those day's it was achieved by getting newspaper or brown paper bags putting the clothes under the mattress, covering them with the paper and then sleeping on it.

Whilst in the care system I was moved around to various places subjected to racial, mental and physical abuse by the staff and other children.

In a school run by nuns, I had a fight by a girl who called me a black wog, we had a fight and I ripped out hair to the scalp, leaving it bald empty and smooth.

The nuns paraded me around with the hair in a plastic bag informing everyone "look what Lissette has done; she is possessed by the devil".

I was returned back to the care home and the staff locked me in a room for the rest of the day until the devil came out of me.

I was so glad I had my brother who was there to protect me, if I told him. During this time, I would go and visit my mum and siblings on the weekend in Enfield and found it very difficult to leave them knowing what I was leaving them to but I had no choice, I could not take them with me.

I left the care home at seventeen and decided to live in Enfield, but left after two weeks due to it being over crowded as all five of us were living at mums plus my brother's girlfriend and there were many arguments. Also, me and mum were not getting on I did not really know her; we were like strangers and I disliked her behaviour.

I was very happy my mother gave up drinking in the end and we attended a few Alcoholics Anonymous meetings, where I met a celebrity amongst the group who was in a very famous band at the time.

My mum was very mean and selfish when it came to food, even though I did not live at home I could not understand how my mother did not realise that Sharron was only eating biscuits and drinking tea for three years. The food my mum used to cook entailed cow foot, tripe (cows belly), okra, liver and various other types of offal, always served with rice just for herself. That is why I used to come to the house and cook English food, fish fingers, spaghetti Boulogne's, chips and the food I knew she would eat, as she was an anorexic.

Most of my arguments and bouts of violence always revolved around me defending my little siblings, especially Sharron who was always palmed off with our baby sister. For instance, on my twenty fifth birthday party, my mum arrived with my little sister, a cake and Sharron came with her friends from college. It was an elaborate affair with Champagne, a music sound group and very expensive invitations from Saatchi and Saatchi which was a gift from an upstairs neighbour from ponders end.

During part of the celebrations, Sharron decided she wanted to leave with her friends and go out. She told mum her plans, which, Mum, said she was fine to go but she had to take her little sister with her. On hearing this conversation, I stepped in and said to my mum "my little sister is your responsibility not Sharron's, she came with you therefore she should leave with you". I also stated, "It was you that brought her into the world not Sharron's. All I remember is a violent out burst from my mother, being slapped in the face in front of my guests, feeling highly embarrassed, crying with the party coming to an abrupt end.

The cake remained untouched, I returned it in the post and we did not speak for quite a while.

Whilst living at home I got involved with the wrong crowd and became a prolific shoplifter. To make money I would steal to order, including all the top brand names. During one of my sprees, I came across a silk cows neck top, which I stole, loved wearing and the brand was Armani. I loaned it to one of my brothers, even though it was many sizes too small, due to his buff stature, but he still wanted it. What brother wanted he got. After asking him several times for my top, he refused. My own jumper, I had to wait for it to go into the laundry to get it back. A big argument and fight ensued in which he put his foot in it and literally tore it in half, the rest is history.

Soon after a brother became involved in a serious incident, which resulted in me having to go as a witness to the Old Bailey, which I found extremely hard because I was young and scared, seeing all the judges in wigs knowing it was a big court.

Luckily, due to my brother having a good barrister, defence team and the jury seeing through the lies of the police and the prosecution, my brother was given a lesser sentence as there were exceptional-mitigating circumstances.

Whilst my brother was incarcerated my grandmother died, which had a devastating effect on me as I used to call her "mum" and she was the only face I remember visiting me during my many stays in care. She always provided food for the house in Enfield when she could, and she was the first person I would visit on my weekends when I was released from care.

I got a flat in Stamford hill where I remained until the age of thirty-two living in a one bedroom flat. I do remember giving Sharron a key and would often come home from work and find her there with a bunch of school friends, which I did not mind as I knew she had somewhere to escape to.

I had several failed and violent relationships but I did have one that was positive in that I had my daughter. Unfortunately, when that ended I had another partner, where it escalated to a period of drug addiction, which left me with no option but to put myself into a Rehabilitation program, leave London and start afresh keeping my daughter with me.

I went to rehab in 1998 and relocated to Hampshire, during one of the group narcotics anonymous meetings I met a very famous female presenter, who later died of a suicide over dose. I am still clean today and my daughter is a thriving twenty three year old beautiful young woman.

I wanted to contribute to this book for several reasons being, I feel guilty, as I did not treat Sharron very nice as a child and having to leave them both there with my mum. And, also I believe due to my mum's behaviour, I have had no childhood and behave and do things to excess, which includes trust, cleaning, over protectiveness, confusing sex with love and being very mothering.

I have found it difficult being away from London, even though it was the best thing I ever done. I do go back and visit most of my siblings and they visit me too.

My journey has been challenging but I feel that if I had not been through certain things I would not be the person I am today.

I have not had much of a career but I am a good mother and seek for my success and happiness in the future. I am also very proud of what Sharron has achieved considering where she has come from and who she had to learn from. I have been with Sharron from the beginning when she expressed she loved acting. I have always had faith in her and knew she could achieve anything she wanted if she put her mind to it.

I am very overwhelmed with the play "Femmetamorphosis" that she has written, and very proud and honoured that Sharron has trusted and involved me, even though she knows I am not experienced in that field of work, she still wanted me to be her right hand for which I am very grateful.

Considering the play started off in Leicester square as a showcase and then to be told she has 26 shows (I had no clue what fringe was) at the Edinburgh fringe festival I was very surprised how quick everything unfolded. Whilst at the Edinburgh fringe festival it was stressful, tiring and a very draining experience but I still loved it.

I saw many plays and it is a beautiful place, which, I thoroughly enjoyed and will be back again.

I told her "Those that called you the black rat, you can now say the ugly duckling has turned into a beautiful swan". Look at what she has achieved now, with determination and a bit of balls she can get what she wants, she is still on her journey, continuing.

All those that doubted her, "what have you accomplished, have you done any better and where are you now?".

My Stepdad Tony

This was probably one of the most painful chapters to complete but in the interest of fairness and the longing to get some real answers about our fractured relationship I met with Tony not having seen him in years, but did mention to him a year ago, that I was intending to write a book and would welcome his input. Therefore, here is his account:

"I first met Yvonne in the local pub we had a few drinks and we both liked to puff. A few weeks later, my mate John said he had seen Yvonne and that she had been asking for me. At that time, I had been seeing a nice Irish woman, then a few days later I bumped into Yvonne in the street and she had two kids with her, Sharron was holding buggy whilst the baby was in the pushchair.

Then we met unexpectedly without the children and we went to the pub had a few drinks, she never refused a free drink especially in the Horse and Dray pub. I walked her home and I give her a kiss goodnight, she was a very attractive woman.

From that evening, we kept on meeting and was not intimate for some time.

The relationship progressed from friendship and I got to meet the two other children that were in care, Yvonne never told me what happened and I never felt the need to question it further, I sensed it was a delicate sensitive situation. The house was always full of people and arguments between the siblings were a major feature.

She would sometimes get drunk and I do recollect one evening the police had met her, expressing she was drunk and disorderly and they were about to arrest her and take her away, however I explained that I was her boyfriend and they let me take her home. After that particular incident, I warned her she needed to sort herself out.

I often ended up carrying her home on my shoulders from her friend's parties or a night out at the pub. We got together at time when black and white couples was a rarity and frowned upon.

I thought a lot of Yvonne when I was with her but she would have tantrums and break crockery. In the end, I think I convinced her to go, I decided she had to something, Alcoholics Anonymous and she eventually stopped drinking.

I would go fishing and bring the fish back for Yvonne to cook she was great in the kitchen, I enjoyed her black pudding, pepper pot, fish cake, sous, she made good food.

We had a keen interest in gardening, growing vegetables in an allotment and her small garden.

On one occasion Yvonne, myself and the two girls went to Notting hill carnival and the youngest one got lost, worried sick we went to look for her and found them both hours later with a room full of lost children.

I favoured the little one more as I felt Sharron never liked me as a white man, and we never really got on. The youngest one was friendlier and open, where Sharron was cold, guarded and standoffish. Years later, when they became adults I went to see them both starring in a play together.

I recall Sharron was always waiting for her mother to return and I would tell her "she's not coming home get yourself ready for bed no good standing at the window". She would be asking me why her mum weren't there and I remember her say "I hate her".

At some stage during our relationship, her interests changed and she began to go bingo on a regular basis, which I did not like along with selling food in pubs and Shabeen's as I never knew who she would meet nor whom she was with. When she took to the road that was her business.

When she did win at the bingo I never understood why she would still purchase second hand clothes, even wearing some of the trousers inside out. And then I wondered about her mental health.

We had our time together and departed after twenty-two years. Since the separation, she has been diagnosed with Dementia and being looked after in residential care. I will not visit, as

I would like to remember her as she was but I am in contact with her daughters and the grandchildren. The youngest daughter I love she calls me dad and her kids call me grandad.

I have the greatest respect for them both especially Sharron knowing the pain she went through. We are fine now it is not that bad we have cleared up the past and this book will help her to heal.

Epilogue

I started writing this book in November 2014 whilst in counselling for Post-Traumatic Stress Disorder (PTSD). I was diagnosed whilst looking after Yvonne who is currently in a residential care home with Dementia. Every time I went to visit her, I would get flashbacks about what I had experienced in my childhood, which were very distressing, and I did know why it was happening because I had blocked it out of memory, or so I thought. It was talking with my therapist that it came out how bad I was let down by the local services, neighbours, schools and the council. What you need to know is that people saw what was going on and chose to do nothing. I was telling agencies about the neglect and abuse to which I was ignored. The local authority failed in their duty to protect a child. Social services should have taken more action and were negligent in not removing me from the home where all the abuse was happening. Through a solicitor, I have written to all the agencies who claim that they have no records of me, at all, none.

The last time I saw my biological mother was in 2017, and I am currently seeking to sue the council.

Writing this has been hard on some of the family who wanted me to keep it quiet and in the past, no point in raking up old news so I only speak to a few members now as I respect their wishes as they should respect mine.

I am focused on my well-being, career and writing with no incentive for a relationship, choosing to stay single for the foreseeable future.

In the autumn, I will be writing a screenplay for television and the sequel to the stage comedy Femmetamorphosis.

Organisations and useful Helplines.

Beat provides helplines for adults and young people offering support and information about eating disorders and difficulties with food, weight and shape.

Beating Eating Disorders

Adult helpline: 0845 634 1414 or

Email: **help@b-eat.co.uk**

Youthline: 0845 634 7650 or

Email: **fyp@b-eat.co.uk**

Website: **www.b-eat.co.uk**

Eating Disorders Support an organisation providing help and support to anyone affected by an eating problem such as anorexia nervosa, bulimia nervosa or binge eating. It also provides help for those who are caring for, or supporting someone with an eating disorder.

Eating Disorders Support Helpline:

01494 793 223

Email:

support@eatingdisorderssupport.co.uk

Website:

www.eatingdisorderssupport.co.uk

Mind provides advice and support to empower anyone experiencing a mental health problem.

Mind

Infoline: 0300 123 3393

Text: 86463

Email: **info@mind.org.uk**

Website: **www.mind.org.uk**

CALM

CALM is the Campaign Against Living Miserably, for men aged 15-35

Phone: 0800 58 58 58

Website: **www.thecalmzone.net**

YoungMinds

Information on child and adolescent mental health. Service for parents and professionals.

Phone: Parents' helpline (Mon-Fri, 9:30am-4pm) 0808 802 5544

Website: **www.youngminds.org.uk**

Samaritans supports anyone in distress, around the clock, through 201 branches across the UK and Republic of Ireland.

Samaritans

Helpline: 08457 90 90 90

Email: **jo@samaritans.org**

Website: **www.samaritans.org**

National Self Harm Network has a forum and provides support for individuals who self-harm to reduce emotional distress and improve the quality of life.

National Self Harm Network

Website: ***www.nshn.co.uk***

Self Injury Support is a national organisation that supports girls and women affected by self-injury or self-harm.

Self Injury Support

Tess text support: 07800 0472 908 (Text and Support for girls and young women under 25 years old)

Women's Helpline: 0808 800 8088 (Open Wednesday from 7pm-9pm and Thursdays 3-5pm)

Website: **www.selfinjurysupport.org.uk**

National Domestic Violence Helpline is a 24-hour national free phone help line offering support, help and information for women experiencing domestic violence.

National Domestic Violence Helpline

Helpline: 0808 2000 247 (open 24hrs run in partnership with Women's Aid and Refuge **www.refuge.org.uk**

Website: **www.nationaldomesticviolencehelpline.org.uk**

Women's Aid is the national charity for women and children working to end domestic violence.

Women's Aid

Helpline: 0808 2000 247

Email: **helpline@womensaid.org.uk**

Website: **www.womensaid.org.uk**

OCD Action is a confidential helpline and information service offering help, information and support for people with OCD, carers and anyone concerned that they, or their friends or relatives, may have OCD or related disorder.

OCD Action

Helpline: 0845 390 6232 (open 9:30am-5pm Monday – Friday)

Email: **support@ocdaction.org.uk**

Website: **www.ocdaction.org.uk**

OCD-UK is a charity, which provides information on OCD and related conditions, as well as therapy and treatment resources.

OCD-UK

Advice Line: 0845 120 3778 (open 9:00am-5pm Monday – Friday)

Email: **support@ocduk.org**

Website: **www.ocduk.org**

Get Connected is the UK's free, confidential helpline service for young people under 25 years old who need help, but do not know where to turn.

Get Connected

Free Helpline: 0808 808 4994 (open from 1pm-11pm very day)

Text: 80849

Website: **www.getconnected.org.uk**

ChildLine is a 24 counselling service for children and young people offering support, advice and help on a wide range of issues.

ChildLine

ChildLine: 0800 11 11 (anytime)

Website: **www.childline.org.uk**

National Society for the Prevention of Cruelty to Children (NSPCC) is a charity campaigning and working in child protection.

National Society for the Prevention of Cruelty to Children

Helpline: 0808 800 5000

Email: **help@nspcc.org.uk**

Website: **www.nspcc.org.uk**

The National Association for the People Abused in Childhood is a UK supporting adults who, have been abused in childhood.

The National Association for the People Abused in Childhood
Support line: 0808 801 0331
Email: **support@napac.org.uk**
Website: www.napac.org.uk

Sharron Hope was born in London and is the founder of StarS Beauty Spot and Drama, a community based organisation that works with young people and women. The organisation has given opportunity to a variety of service users of all ages. She is also an anti-knife crime activist and educational speaker.

As an Actress and Playwright, she has toured her play Femmetamorphosis both in London and at the Edinburgh festival.

Printed in Great
Britain
by Amazon